HURRICANE DISASTERS

John Hawkins

W

FRANKLIN WATTS
LONDON • SYDNEY

First published in 2012 by Franklin Watts

Copyright © 2012 Arcturus Publishing Limited

Franklin Watts
338 Euston Road
London NW1 3BH

Franklin Watts Australia
Level 17/207 Kent Street, Sydney NSW 2000

Produced by Arcturus Publishing Limited,
26/27 Bickels Yard, 151–153 Bermondsey Street, London SE1 3HA

Text: John Hawkins
Editors: Joe Harris and Penny Worms
Design: Graham Rich
Cover design: Graham Rich

Picture credits:
Corbis: cover, 1, 4, 7, 12, 14, 15, 16, 19, 20, 23, 30b, 32b, 34, 37, 38, 40, 43, 44t, 45t, 45c, 45bc, 45b. Getty: 10b, 24b, 25, 27, 28, 29, 44tc, 44b. NASA: 5, 8, 45tc. Science Photo Library: 9, 41. Shutterstock: 10t, 18, 24t, 26, 30t, 32t, 36, 44c. TopFoto: 6, 44bc. Wikimedia: 22.

Cover image: Miami, Florida. Palm trees on a beach are buffeted by Hurricane Georges in September 1998.

A CIP catalogue record for this book is available from the British Library.

Dewey Decimal Classification Number 363.3′4922

ISBN 978 1 4451 1017 2

Printed in China

Franklin Watts is a division of Hachette Children's Books, an Hachette UK company.
www.hachette.co.uk

SL001927EN
Supplier 03, Date 0112, Print Run 1425

Contents

What Is a Hurricane?

A hurricane is a furious, spiralling tropical storm that roars in from the ocean and lashes the coast, causing terrible damage. It can smash buildings apart and hurl trees and cars into the air. The wind can reach speeds of more than 250 kph (155 mph) and brings with it torrential rain and thunderstorms.

WHAT'S IN A NAME?

A severe tropical storm is classed as a hurricane if it has winds that blow faster than 118 kph (73 mph). In the Americas, people call them hurricanes after the ancient Mayan god of wind and storms, Hurakan. In Southeast Asia, people call them typhoons, from the Chinese 'Taifeng', meaning 'great wind'. In India and Australia, they are called cyclones.

Sand whips through a car park as Hurricane Ike hits Texas in 2005.

PARTS OF A HURRICANE

All hurricanes share the same features. The destructive part is the whirling band of wind and rainstorms. However, in the centre, there is a still area with very low air pressure called the 'eye'. The air pressure is so low that warm air and water are drawn up into the hurricane, continually feeding it.

SIZE OF A HURRICANE

A hurricane can extend 18 km (11 miles) upward. Widths vary, but a large hurricane can be 480 km (nearly 300 miles) wide. Some typhoons have measured 1,290 km (over 800 miles) across!

This satellite image shows Hurricane Isabel near Puerto Rico in the Caribbean.

SAFFIR-SIMPSON HURRICANE SCALE

This is the scale used for reporting the size of hurricanes, based on the wind speed. At lower speeds, they are called tropical storms.

Category	Speed (kph)	Speed (mph)	Damage
1	119–153	74–95	Little damage to buildings; coastal flooding
2	154–177	96–110	Damage to roofs, doors and windows; flood damage to piers; some trees blown down
3	178–209	111–130	Structural damage to small buildings; large trees blown down; coastal and inland flooding; flood damage to small structures
4	210–249	131–155	Roofs lost from small buildings; serious erosion of beach areas; inland flooding
5	Over 249	Over 156	Roofs lost from all buildings; some buildings destroyed or blown away; serious flood damage to all structures near the coast

Where Hurricanes Happen

Tropical storms occur in tropical regions of the Atlantic, Indian and Pacific Oceans. The water temperature must be at least 26.5 °C (79.7 °F) for the storm to be able to gather enough strength to be classed as a hurricane. Most Atlantic hurricanes form off the west coast of Africa, then drift westward to reach land in Central America and the Caribbean.

Rescuers save a baby from raging flood waters near Guayama in the Caribbean after Hurricane Hortense in 1996.

LANDFALL

When a hurricane, cyclone or typhoon reaches land, it causes destruction along the coast and continues its path inland. After hitting land, the storm rapidly loses power as it is no longer heated by tropical seas. Within 12 hours most of the force has been spent – though it can travel as far as 280 km (175 miles) inland before dying out.

STORM ZONES

The most destructive hurricanes strike the southeastern coast of the United States, Central America and the Caribbean. Typhoons plague the coasts around the Indian Ocean and many parts of the Pacific Ocean.

Violent seas batter the shore in Jamaica as Hurricane Gilbert makes landfall in 1988.

In the Indian Ocean, they strike Indonesia, India, Sri Lanka and Thailand, but can hit Madagascar and east Africa, too. In the Pacific they are most common around Japan, eastern China and the Philippines, but can also strike the west coast of Australia and New Guinea. Their impact is greatest in areas where the most people live.

HEAVIEST HIT

The Caroline and Marianas island chains in the Pacific and Luzon Island in the Philippines have the largest number of tropical storms of anywhere in the world, with around ten each year. Mozambique in Africa depends on the rain brought by tropical storms to boost its water supplies, but the country frequently floods as a result.

How Hurricanes Happen

A tropical storm builds up over the sea where equatorial winds from different directions meet. The warm air spirals upward, taking heat and moisture from the sea. The spiral gathers speed and strength.

A colour-coded map based on satellite images shows the variation in sea temperature around the globe.

DRAWING IN POWER

An Atlantic hurricane begins as a thunderstorm off the west coast of Africa and then becomes a tropical depression. This is a system of swirling clouds and rain, with winds of less than 62 kph (39 mph). Warm air, carrying evaporated water, rises from the sea's surface. The air cools as it rises, and the water vapour condenses to form rain clouds, which add to the growing storm. Heat escapes from the condensing water and warms the air higher up, which rises in turn. This creates a cycle of warm air being sucked up from the ocean, losing its water to storm clouds, and warming more air. The rising column pulls more and more warm air and water from the surface of the sea.

COLLIDING WINDS

Winds from different directions collide and circle around the column of rising air and moisture, setting up a circular wind pattern. Much higher up is a stronger wind, blowing in a single direction and carrying the warm air away. This action pulls up yet more air. High air pressure above the storm helps to suck in more air at the bottom where the air pressure is low. The wind speed increases, first to tropical storm strength, between 55 to 118 kph (34 to 73 mph) and finally to hurricane force.

Clouds swirl around the eye wall of Hurricane Katrina in 2005.

HURRICANE WINDS

Storms whip around in a hurricane at speeds of up to 250 kph (155 mph), or even 320 kph (200 mph) in a very severe Pacific typhoon. The winds in a hurricane circle counterclockwise in the northern hemisphere and clockwise in the southern hemisphere. This is because of the effect of the spinning of the earth on the movement of the wind and cloud.

Hurricane Katrina, 2005

New Orleans is a unique city. It is the home of jazz music, Mardi Gras and delicious Creole and Cajun cooking. Its relaxed atmosphere stems from a fusion of French, Spanish and African–American influences. But its situation on the hurricane-prone coast of the Gulf of Mexico makes it vulnerable. Many people were horrified but not in fact surprised when disaster struck on 29 August 2005.

The flood defences outside New Orleans are overwhelmed by the storm surge.

WATER, WATER EVERYWHERE

New Orleans is a low-lying metropolis on the Gulf Coast. To the south is the vast Mississippi River. To the north lies Lake Pontchartrain. The city is surrounded by water. A system of levees (dykes) and canals was built to protect the parts of the city lying below the water level. Everyone knew that if the levees were breached, the consequences for the half million inhabitants of New Orleans would be dire.

HIGH WIND FRENZY

On 26 August 2005, in the Gulf of Mexico, Hurricane Katrina was building up to a Category-5 hurricane. It was a frenzy of high winds and rain, on a path heading close to New Orleans. Those residents with a car and sufficient cash joined the traffic leaving the city. However, many people stayed at home.

LANDFALL

Katrina made landfall in Mississippi as a Category-3 hurricane, with winds up to 200 kph (125 mph). Hopes that New Orleans would miss the worst effects were dashed when storm surges burst through several levees, emptying the waters of canals leading from Lake Pontchartrain into the streets. Thousands of residents were now in peril from severe flooding.

WHY IT HAPPENED

A storm surge is the result of high winds pushing on the ocean's surface towards the shore. This surge in water combines with the normal tide and builds into a storm tide, raising the sea level considerably. Katrina pushed a wall of water almost 9 m (29 feet) over the New Orleans levees. There had been warnings. Two years before, an article in *Civil Engineering Magazine* warned that some of the levees were 'rudimentary' and insufficient for the task. Nothing was done.

RISING WATERS

The flood waters rose above first- and then second-floor levels of people's homes, forcing them into their attics or onto rooftops. Electricity and telephone networks went down and the waters quickly became polluted. Within hours, citizens of the richest country in the world had no power, no fresh water or food, and were at risk from fire, dehydration and disease. The horror went on, street after street, covering the poorest neighbourhoods across the city.

A couple and their baby escape from their car in floods caused by Katrina.

WHERE'S THE HELP?

The authorities were slow to act at first, as if they were frozen by horror. Up to 80 per cent of the city was underwater and there were many dead bodies. Emotional pleas for help from the victims were broadcast on television but there was little evidence of an organized aid effort.

THE SUPERDOME

The Superdome football stadium sheltered as many as 10,000 people during the storm. Afterwards it became a refuge for others expecting to find food and shelter while they waited for evacuation. Unfortunately, those people discovered that there were few supplies, and living conditions were horrible. They had been promised fleets of buses to escape the mayhem, but these did not arrive. People who had already suffered the destruction of their worldly possessions became increasingly desperate and scared. Some argued that the slow response by the authorities was because the victims were largely poor.

LAWLESSNESS

Both at the Superdome and elsewhere people began relaying tales of lawlessness. There were stories of gunshots, violence and looting. Later, it became clear that much of the looting was people taking much-needed food.

EYEWITNESS

Tony Zumbado, a photojournalist for the TV network NBC, went to the New Orleans Convention Center. 'There is nothing offered to [the people there]. No water, no ice, no rations, nothing for the last four days. They were told to go to the Convention Center. They've been behaving. They've been supportive of one another. But what I've seen there, I've never seen in this country... I saw two people die in front of me of dehydration. I saw a baby near death. There's no police. No authority.'

Hurricane Katrina, 2005

Fire and water: A fireman helps a man out of floodwaters as a home burns in New Orleans.

THE PRESIDENT ACTS

Perhaps because New Orleans had a reputation for violence, the National Guard arrived in numbers to protect empty, wrecked businesses. This happened at a time when people remained trapped and the bodies of the dead remained uncollected. Two days after the hurricane, President George W Bush ended his vacation and on 2 September he travelled to New Orleans to see the devastation for himself. When he returned, he signed a $10.5 billion emergency funding bill and announced he was sending 7,000 more troops to the disaster zone. Many thought it was too little, too late.

EVACUATION

A week after the catastrophe, the mayor of New Orleans, Ray Nagin, ordered the evacuation of the city to prevent infection and disease. Most people left but some refused – for example, because they were unwilling to leave pets behind. Americans across the 50 states offered their homes and funds to New Orleanians who had lost everything.

THE HUMAN COST

The retrieval of bodies began some 10 days after the disaster. The death toll, although tragically high, was less than expected. More than 1,800 people died throughout Louisiana and Mississippi, most of them in and around New Orleans.

PUMPS IN ACTION

The storm waters had swamped the city's pumps, put in place to clear the city of water. It was days before they were repaired and back in action. Fortunately, it took less time than predicted to clear the flooded city – despite the arrival of other hurricanes.

LEARNING FROM CATASTROPHES

Later, after analyzing what had happened, experts said that Katrina was a much more complex hurricane than the flood protection system had been designed to stop. Katrina had been the equivalent of four storms battering the area in different ways. Assessing the failings of the system was vital in planning a new system for a rebuilt New Orleans.

This satellite image shows the extent of the flooding.

THE FINANCIAL COST

Hurricane Katrina ranks as one of the most costly natural disasters to hit the United States. It cost insurance companies $70 billion. However, many people were uninsured. The total cost of damage was much more than that.

THE POLITICAL COST

There was widespread criticism of the state and federal responses to Katrina even as the clean-up operation began. The government's slow response caused political outrage. It damaged President Bush's reputation and made many people lose faith in his administration.

A soldier looks down into flooded streets, searching for survivors in the aftermath of Katrina.

FIVE YEARS ON

The situation slowly stabilized in the region as federal and local agencies restored order and aid began to flow into the area. Within two weeks, people began to return, initially to salvage their belongings and later to rebuild their lives. By 2010, 90 per cent had returned. Building projects had helped many to rebuild their homes or build new ones. Unemployment in the city was lower than the national average and it was one of the fastest growing cities in America.

On the fifth anniversary, President Barack Obama said: 'We all remember it keenly – water pouring through broken levees; mothers holding their children above the waterline; people stranded on rooftops begging for help; and bodies lying in the streets of a great American city. It was a natural disaster but also a man-made catastrophe; a shameful breakdown in government that left countless men and women and children abandoned and alone.... But thanks to you... the great people of this great city, New Orleans is blossoming again.'

LEARNING FROM CATASTROPHES

The city's flood defences are now fortified with stronger levees, steel-reinforced concrete walls and huge flood gates that will grind shut when floods threaten. The pump stations have flood-proof safehouses so operators won't have to evacuate as they did in 2005. But even though the city is far better protected, experts warn of new risks in the future. One threat is climate change, which is thought to be responsible for the rise of global sea levels and increased hurricane activity in the Gulf of Mexico.

GALVESTON

Galveston, 1900

On 4 September 1900, the US Weather Bureau issued a storm warning. A 'tropical storm disturbance moving northward over Cuba' was thought to be heading for Florida. The people of Galveston, Texas, some 1,600 km (1,000 miles) away were pleased to get some cooler weather after the stifling heat of the previous days, but the storm was about to take a nasty turn.

FLORIDA LANDFALL

Two days after the Weather Bureau's warning, the storm hit Florida, causing extensive flooding. It then veered to the west, out over the open waters of the Gulf of Mexico. The next morning, Isaac Cline, director of the weather station at Galveston, received a message from Washington to hoist storm-warning flags. The wind was blowing at 27 kph (17 mph).

BRIGHT AND BREEZY

Most Galvestonians took no notice of the storm-warning flags. Vacationers packed the beaches, enjoying the cool breeze from the sea. The sky remained clear but the barometer was falling. A reporter for the *Galveston News* wrote that the storm had 'changed its course or spent its force before reaching Texas'. He could not have been more wrong.

This illustration depicts the horror of the storm surge in Galveston.

RAISING THE ALARM

Isaac Cline's brother, Joseph, who was chief clerk of the weather station, woke on 8 September at 4 am to find water in the back yard. That meant that the tide had risen 1.5 m (5 feet) above normal. Joseph returned to the weather station, while Isaac roused the neighbours. A few had the good sense to leave their homes and head for higher ground, but most were not alarmed. Galveston was built on a sand bar and flooded frequently.

NAMING SYSTEM

The practice of naming hurricanes started during World War II (1939–45). Only female names were used, but this changed in 1978. The World Meteorological Organization draws up alphabetical lists of names for both Atlantic and Pacific storms. Storms are named when they have winds of more than 62 kph (39 mph). Once a name has been used for a major hurricane, it is not employed again.

TRAPPED

At 8.45 am it began to rain and Joseph Cline received a message from Washington to say that the storm had changed direction from northwest to northeast. He went to change the storm-warning flags but found they had been ripped from the flagpoles. By noon, people were being lashed with rain as they headed for higher ground. They soon realized that the causeways connecting Galveston to the mainland had been washed away.

Men used ropes to pull away the debris of houses, looking for bodies.

CUT OFF

By 2.30 pm, the weather station's rain gauge had been blown away. Joseph tried to send a message to Washington only to find that the telegraph lines were down. He managed to send a message to nearby Houston. Soon after, that line went down too and Galveston was cut off from the outside world.

VIOLENT WINDS

By 5.30 pm, the weather station's wind gauge had been blown away, after registering wind speeds of over 160 kph (100 mph). Slate tiles torn from the city's roofs were flying through the air with enough force to take a person's head off. The barometer was still dropping. Fifty neighbours took refuge in the Clines' house, which was considered one of the strongest around. Another thousand packed into the Tremont Hotel because it was at one of the highest points of the city. By 6 pm, the front desk was underwater. The wind was gusting to an estimated 190 kph (118 mph) and blowing whole buildings away. At 6.30 pm, the city was then hit by a storm surge up to 1.2 m (4 feet) high, which demolished many of the remaining houses.

 **EYEWITNESS**

In a report written by Isaac Cline after the hurricane, he said:
'By 8 pm a number of houses had drifted up and lodged to the east and southeast of my residence, and these with the force of the waves acted as a battering ram against which it was impossible for any building to stand for any length of time. At 8.30 pm, my residence went down.... Among the lost was my wife, who never rose above the water after the wreck of the building. I was nearly drowned and became unconscious, but recovered through being crushed by timbers and found myself clinging to my youngest child.'

VORTEX

At 10 pm, the hurricane's vortex hit. By that time, the sea level in the city was 4.6 m (15 feet) above the high-tide mark. The wind then turned to the south. Its force dropped, but the ebbing water still had enough strength to rip buildings from their foundations and carry them out into the Gulf.

Men carry away bodies from the wreckage. Most of the bodies were piled onto tugs and buried at sea.

LOOTERS

The authorities declared martial law and six looters were shot on sight. One reportedly had 23 severed ring-fingers in his pocket.

The new sea wall in Galveston is shown here, nine years after the terrible storm.

SURVIVORS AND THE DEAD

It is estimated that some 6,000 Galvestonians died in the storm, along with another 4,000 to 6,000 along the Texas coast. The property damage was $400 million at today's prices. Hundreds of people died when a church they had taken refuge in collapsed on top of them. More than 100 patients died in a city hospital and 87 of the 90 children at St Mary's Orphanage perished. One woman was washed out to sea in a wooden bath. However, she returned safely on the next morning's tide.

LEARNING FROM CATASTROPHES

In 1904, a defensive sea wall, 4.8 km (3 miles) long and 5 m (17 feet) high, was built along the sea front at Galveston. It has since been extended to 16 km (10 miles). Behind it were the remaining 2,156 buildings, including St Patrick's Church. These were jacked up and the area was filled with millions of tonnes of sand. The church alone weighed nearly 3,000 tonnes. The city was raised by as much as 5 m (17 feet) in places. These measures have served to protect the residents of Galveston for more than 100 years.

Typhoon Vera, 1959

On 26 September 1959, Typhoon Vera was heading towards Honshu, the largest of Japan's islands, with winds of up to 258 kph (160 mph). There was no panic because Japan is hit by three or four typhoons every year and there was five days' warning. Flights in and out of the area were cancelled. However, the inhabitants simply put up storm shutters, bought food and water, and waited.

SURGE TIDE

Nagoya, Japan's third largest city, has a population of 1.3 million. In September 1959, it lay directly in the typhoon's path. The typhoon struck late on Saturday night when the tide was high. A wall of water 5 m (17 feet) high crashed into the city, battering the sea walls and dykes with incredible force. The water levelled any building in its way.

US Navy ships made food drops to survivors.

Whole houses were literally moved by Typhoon Vera.

FLOODS

The city flooded. Winds tore the roofs off houses and hurled deadly debris across the city. Twenty-one ships were beached – seven of them ocean-going vessels. Logs from timber yards battered buildings.

NO HELP

Within three hours the typhoon had moved on, leaving Nagoya flooded and full of dead bodies. No help came from Tokyo, as Vera had also caused havoc there. The survivors were soon famished. The US Navy dropped food and supplies, but a week later, there were still 25,000 people trapped on their rooftops.

DEATH TOLL

Vera's official death toll was 5,000. However, hundreds of people were swept away and never found. About 40,000 homes were destroyed, leaving 1.5 million people homeless. In all, there was over $2 billion worth of damage.

LEARNING FROM CATASTROPHES

After Vera, the Japanese government enacted a law requiring the drawing up and execution of disaster prevention plans. It was also decided that 1 September would be 'Disaster Prevention Day'. On this day, every year, both the emergency services and the people of Japan take part in drills and evacuations to ensure they are prepared for any emergency.

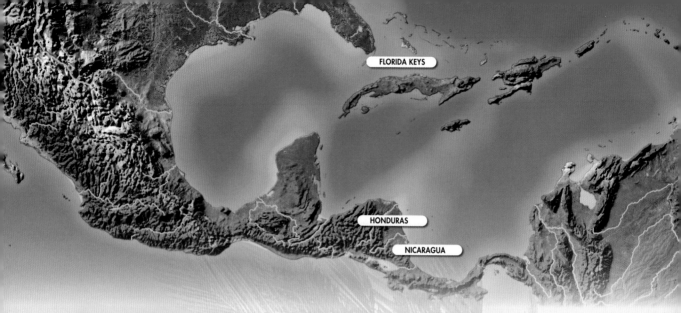

FLORIDA KEYS

HONDURAS

NICARAGUA

Hurricane Mitch, 1998

On 21 October 1998, a tropical depression formed in the southern Caribbean Sea. The following day, it was given the name Mitch. Over the next five days, Mitch strengthened to a Category-5 hurricane. It was the strongest hurricane in the Caribbean in a decade and the fourth strongest ever recorded in the Atlantic.

WILD WINDS

Mitch's winds reached a peak of 290 kph (180 mph) on 26 October as it reached the coast of Honduras. It sustained its Category-5 status for a staggering 33 hours. By the morning of 28 October, the winds had dropped to 195 kph (120 mph). It stalled for more than two days off the Honduras coast.

FLOODS

On October 30, Mitch moved across Honduras and Nicaragua. The slow drift meant that rains increased causing terrible flooding and mudslides. Bridges, roads and buildings were destroyed. Whole villages were swept away in the fast-moving torrents of mud and water that came down the mountains.

Popular resorts in the Gulf of Mexico were evacuated in the face of the hurricane's onslaught.

WIDESPREAD DESTRUCTION

Countries that were badly affected included Guatemala, El Salvador and Belize. Nicaragua's official death toll was almost 3,000. Costa Rica and Mexico also suffered.

However, Honduras was the worst hit, with over 5,600 dead and thousands more missing. In all, it is thought that more than 11,000 people died and up to three million survivors were displaced.

 EYEWITNESS

Laura Arriola de Guity was found 80 km (50 miles) out into the Caribbean Sea, almost a week after being thrown from the roof of her home as it was swept out to sea. She said, 'At that moment, there was no difference between the rain, the river, and the ocean. I was still holding my baby and then the sea took him from my hands.' Their home was 3 km (2 miles) from the sea. Laura survived by building a makeshift raft and eating floating pineapples and coconuts. The bodies of her husband and daughter were found later. Her two sons were never found. 'I have nothing. I have nowhere to go,' she said. 'I lost it all.'

Hurricane Mitch, 1998

HEADING TO FLORIDA

Hurricane Mitch wasn't finished yet. Weakened but still on the move, it travelled north, emerging over the warm waters of the Gulf of Mexico and picking up speed again. On 4 November, Mitch hit the west coast of Florida with winds still gusting to nearly 130 kph (80 mph). Hardest hit were the Florida Keys, where tornadoes flipped mobile homes, felled trees and snapped power lines. It was devastating for a region that was still recovering from Hurricane Georges, which had battered or destroyed 4,000 homes only six weeks before.

The town of Morolica in Honduras was destroyed as the Rio Grande overcame flood defences that had stood for 200 years.

Nothing could stand in the face of Mitch's 290 kph (180 mph) winds.

THE HURRICANES OF 1998

Hurricane Mitch made its appearance during the 1998 Atlantic hurricane season – the deadliest in more than 200 years. Not since the Great Hurricane struck Barbados and Martinique in 1780 had the Atlantic region seen so many storm-related deaths. In 1998 there were 14 tropical storms, of which 10 became hurricanes. Three of these became major hurricanes. In the four-year period between 1995 and 1998 there were a total of 33 hurricanes, an all-time record.

DYING OUT

Mitch also hit south and central Florida. Some 19 cm (7.5 inches) of rain flooded streets in Miami and tornadoes damaged houses. The Bahamas were lashed with high winds and rains before the storm eventually broke up 160 km (100 miles) to the north of the islands.

LETHAL LEGACY

Despite the damage in Florida, Mitch had left its most lethal legacy in the poor third-world countries of Central America. Apart from the tragic loss of life, the President of Honduras claimed the storm had set the country back 50 years.

Hurricane Wilma, 2005

The Atlantic hurricane season of 2005 was the worst ever. There were 15 hurricanes, of which four reached Category-5 status. After Hurricane Katrina in August, the people of the United States were rightly nervous when, in October, another hurricane warning was issued. Hurricane Wilma was heading to Florida.

THE BEGINNING

Wilma began to build in the western Caribbean on 15 October. Four days later, it had grown into the most intense hurricane ever recorded in the Atlantic. Wind speeds were nearly 280 kph (174 mph) and its eye was tiny – only 3–6 km (2–4 miles) wide.

Residents walk through the flooded streets of Playa del Carmen beach resort in Mexico. Howling winds, collapsed buildings and uprooted trees confined thousands of tourists to shelters for three days.

LANDFALL

Wilma first made landfall in the Yucatan Peninsula, a popular tourist destination. For many, their paradise vacation had turned into a nightmare. Even though Wilma had weakened in strength, it grew in size, with hurricane force winds extending 136 km (85 miles) from the eye. An island off the Mexican coast near Cancun recorded rainfall of over 172 cm (68 inches) in 42 hours. Wilma then turned on to a northeasterly track, heading for Florida.

EVACUATION

Many storm-weary Florida residents decided to ignore the warnings to evacuate. There had been previous evacuations but no direct hits. The authorities started to get nervous that the threat was not being taken seriously enough. They warned of power outages and flooding, and urged those who were not moving to stockpile food and water.

AFTER THE STORM

As it turned out, some 6 million people were without power for up to six days. There was major damage, but very few people died. Wilma left the Florida skies cloudless and the temperatures cooler than usual for that time of year. The weather was a blessing. The stifling heatwave that followed Katrina a few months before had compounded the misery for those with no water.

BAROMETRIC PRESSURE

Barometric (air) pressure is one of the best measures of the force of a hurricane, along with its wind speed and size. The more powerful the hurricane, the lower the pressure at the eye. At its peak intensity, Wilma's pressure at the eye was 882 millibars, the lowest ever recorded for an Atlantic hurricane.

Hurricane Andrew, 1992

Hurricane Andrew was one of the most destructive and expensive hurricanes to hit the United States. The small but fierce hurricane slammed into southern Florida on 24 August 1992 at Category-5 strength. It caused property damage of $30 billion and made 250,000 people homeless.

This is a satellite sequence image of Hurricane Andrew's path from 23 August to 25 August as the hurricane moves east to west.

THE BUILD-UP

Andrew started out as a small atmospheric dip in the trade winds from the west coast of Africa. In three days it built into a tropical storm, given the name Andrew because it was the first of the season. By 23 August, it had turned into a Category-4 hurricane heading for the Bahamas.

SMALL BUT DEADLY

Hurricane Andrew hit land in three places – the Bahamas, southern Florida, and south-central Louisiana. At its peak, Andrew was only 145 km (90 miles) in diameter. When it hit Florida, the wind speed was 266 kph (165 mph). As it crossed southern Florida, it left a path of destruction 40 km (25 miles) wide. The area was densely populated with mobile homes and the winds flattened most of them. A storm surge of about 5 m (17 feet) piled boats on top of one another. Communication and power lines fell down.

DAMAGE

The rainfall was low for a hurricane because of its small size and fast, forward movement, so flooding was not extensive. Most of the damage was caused by the winds battering unstable homes at speeds of up to 255 kph (140 mph).

EYEWITNESS

Jim Bossick, a resident of Cutler Ridge in Florida, was guarding a store from looters when he told the *New York Times*, 'I sent my wife off to a shelter,' he said.

'Next time I am going, too. I was hiding in the closet. I'm telling you, I'm never living through one of those things again. I was just scared to death, scared to death.'

Hurricane Andrew, 1992

A NEAR MISS

The path of Hurricane Andrew, as devastating as it was, could have been worse. Although 26 lives were lost and more than 250,000 people were left homeless, many consider it to have been a close shave for the busy city of Miami, only 32 km (20 miles) north. If the storm surge had hit Miami, with its population of 1.9 million, many more lives could have been lost.

HEADING TO LOUISIANA

On 25 August, Hurricane Andrew left Florida and entered the Gulf of Mexico. Weakened over land, Andrew was downgraded to a Category-3 hurricane. It made landfall again in Louisiana a day later. More than a million people had to be evacuated.

TORNADO

In Louisiana, Andrew spawned a tornado that had a damage path 14 km (9 miles) long and 137 m (450 feet) wide. Damage to homes was more severe within the tornado path than that caused by the hurricane in the area. Finally, 11 days after it started, Hurricane Andrew was downgraded to a tropical storm as it drifted northeast.

ENVIRONMENTAL IMPACT

Hurricane Andrew had a terrible impact on the environment. It passed right through the heart of the Everglades, an important wetland area and a national park. There was major damage to mangrove trees, which create a unique wetland habitat. Many other trees suffered damage, too, but those that survived started sprouting new growth within days. In coastal waters, 9.4 million saltwater fish died.

A woman stands guard over her belongings and the remains of her home destroyed by Hurricane Andrew.

LEARNING FROM CATASTROPHES

Hurricane Andrew was the first hurricane to hit Florida in 30 years. It meant that many who lived in its path had not experienced a hurricane before and were not well prepared. Andrew raised awareness and the need for precautions and protection. It had also been a tremendous test for the emergency services. Their actions and evacuation program probably saved a great many lives. South Florida began to improve its building regulations and now they are the strictest in the United States. All new homes have to be built with impact-resistant windows and doors or impact-resistant coverings, such as shutters.

GALVESTON ISLAND

TURKS AND CAICOS

HAITI

CUBA

Hurricane Ike, 2008

The 2008 Atlantic hurricane season was another active season, with eight hurricanes, five of which were at Category-3 strength or above. The most intense and certainly the biggest was Hurricane Ike. At its largest it was almost 1,000 km (600 miles) wide. Ike was blamed for 117 deaths and an estimated $27 billion in damages.

FIRST LANDFALL

Cuba was the first country to be battered by the Category-4 hurricane on 8 September, after a mass evacuation. Eighty per cent of homes on the nearby islands of Turks and Caicos were damaged or destroyed.

HAITI HIT

Next in line was Haiti, a small country that had already suffered at the hands of three previous storms within a month. Ike's arrival was desperately unfortunate for the poor Haitian people. Ike caused catastrophic flooding and killed 61 people.

TEXAS BOUND

The US authorities issued orders for a mandatory evacuation along the coast of Texas and Louisiana. The storm that was heading their way had wind speeds of up to 177 kph (110 mph), but its size meant that a storm surge was likely. The homeland security secretary warned that the storm had 'the potential to produce catastrophic effects'.

Miryam Jacques bails out stinking mud from a family home in Gonaives, Haiti, two weeks after Hurricane Ike caused the river to flood the town.

LOUISIANA

As predicted, there was a storm surge. It hit Louisiana even before Hurricane Ike's arrival in Texas. It flooded areas that had been flooded by Hurricane Gustav only two weeks before.

 ## EYEWITNESS

Miryam Jacques lives in Gonaïves, Haiti's third largest city. It was badly flooded by Hurricane Hanna and then again by Ike. 'Our house is gone and we have nothing left,' she told photographer Gideon Mendel.

'I lost everything in the flood. I have no clothes for my children or myself, and the children must go naked on the roof. They cry and I have no food to give to them. I can do nothing for them.' Miryam's sister drowned in the disaster.

Hurricane Ike, 2008

The outer bands of Hurricane Ike looked like this from the International Space Station.

SHUT DOWN

Texas is the major oil-refining state in the United States. The strength of the impending storm meant that most oil refineries and chemical plants were at risk of damage so they were shut down. As a result, fuel supplies starting dwindling and prices increased. This caused panic buying across the region.

LANDFALL

Ike made landfall over Galveston Island, near Houston in Texas, on 13 September. As predicted, a storm surge caused flooding and extensive damage. Despite repeated warnings – one even saying that people in one-storey houses on Galveston Island faced 'certain death' – some people remained in their homes. Those that managed to survive had to be rescued in a huge search-and-rescue operation.

SENT TO SEA

As Hurricane Ike approached, the *Antalina*, along with other ships in port, were ordered out to sea, where it is easier for a large ship to ride out a hurricane. The *Antalina* planned to skirt around the storm as best it could but it suffered engine loss, meaning it began drifting right into the path of the hurricane. The Coast Guard tried to rescue the crew but the winds were too strong. The crew just had to ride out the storm. It was a tense time for all as communication went dead, but happily all 22 survived. The ship was pulled into port again soon after.

HEADING NORTH

Although weakened after it made landfall, Ike continued on its destructive path north. It caused damage and flooding in Houston and then travelled across the entire country causing havoc. Even Ontario in Canada experienced a record amount of rain.

THE ONE AND ONLY

The World Meteorological Organization decided to retire the name Ike so it will never again be used to name another Atlantic storm.

EYEWITNESS

Dolores Brookshire was a 72-year-old living on the Bolivar Peninsula, a spit of land in Galveston Bay. She had no car and lived with her wheelchair-bound son, Allen. She called her niece as the streets were already flooding. Her niece told the *New York Times*: '[Delores said], "I'm calling you to tell you that I love you and to tell you bye." I said, "Why? Where are you going?" and she said, "Nowhere. Me and Allen are going to drown."' They have not been seen since. Her house is completely gone.

Predicting Hurricanes

Hurricanes are part of the normal weather patterns that happen around the world each year. Hot and cold winds blow at certain times and in certain places. There are also regular patterns to the temperatures of the sea in different areas. Hurricanes happen when certain patterns of wind and sea temperature occur at the same time.

Traffic blocks the highway as people try to escape the path of Hurricane Floyd in Georgia in 1999.

HURRICANE SEASONS

Hurricanes occur when an area of sea is at its warmest. In the northern hemisphere, the hurricane season lasts from June to November. This is when the Caribbean, Central America, North America, Southeast Asia and the Far East are at risk. In the southern hemisphere, the season runs from November to April. This is when south India, Australia and West Africa are at risk.

STUDYING HURRICANES

Meteorologists (people who study the weather) track wind speeds and study satellite photographs of weather systems to help them spot when a hurricane is brewing. They use computer-modelling techniques to predict the likely path of a growing hurricane.

Shop workers board up windows in advance of Hurricane Fran in North Carolina, USA, in 1996.

HELPING PEOPLE TO SAFETY

When a hurricane is expected, governments can warn people to take shelter or move to a safe area. Because weather systems are immensely complex and can change quickly, predictions are not always accurate. Scientists can only predict the wind speeds that will occur on land just before the hurricane hits the coast. Sometimes, it is difficult for governments to decide whether to risk evacuating people needlessly or to leave them where they may be in danger. Evacuation can lead to road traffic accidents, and unnecessary evacuations can make people less likely to take notice of similar warnings in future.

LEARNING FROM CATASTROPHES

After Hurricane Floyd in 1999 caused widespread flooding, the US National Weather Service used the lessons learned to come up with ways to prevent loss of life and property. As floods are the biggest storm-related killer, there are now online tools for local authorities to assess flood risks. They have also implemented a Hurricane Preparedness Week to raise public awareness.

Looking to the Future

Meteorologists monitor sea and wind conditions around the world to help provide early warnings of tropical storms. But even with the best computer-modelling systems, the predictions they make will never be perfect.

This artificially-coloured radar image shows the intensity and direction of the winds in Hurricane Dora in 2005.

LOOKING FOR TROUBLE

Tide gauges show how the swell in the ocean grows as a storm is brewing. Wind gauges measure the speed of the wind, and satellite images reveal the movement and patterns of storm clouds. Information gathered from these instruments can be compared with data from previous hurricanes to help meteorologists predict whether a hurricane is building, where it will go and how powerful it may be when it makes landfall.

HURRICANE HUNTERS

Hurricane hunters are planes that deliberately chase hurricanes, flying as close as possible and even trying to get into the eye of the hurricane and fly with it. They can fly at heights of up to 12 km (7.5 miles). Hurricane hunters carry measuring equipment and also drop instruments attached to parachutes into the storm. New robotic planes that fly without a crew will be able to carry out even more dangerous reconnaissance work.

DANGER AHEAD

Some scientists suggest that hurricanes may become more frequent and damaging in the future because of global warming. If the seas are warmer, the conditions needed for hurricanes to form will occur more often. The number of Category-4 or -5 hurricanes doubled between 1970 and 2005. Over that time, the top part of the sea warmed by 0.5 °C (1 °F).

MORE FLOODS

Scientists also fear that global warming will cause sea levels to rise and more rain to fall. Coastal areas may flood more often and the water could travel further inland. Current storm defences may offer insufficient protection if this proves to be the case.

A hurricane hunter flies into Hurricane Ophelia in 2005.

 ## SOUTH ATLANTIC HURRICANES

In 2004, the first hurricane ever recorded in the South Atlantic rang warning bells for scientists. Because there has never been a hurricane there before, there is no naming system in the South Atlantic. It was unofficially named Catarina as it struck land in Santa Catarina, Brazil. No one knows whether another hurricane will develop there.

Timeline

September 1900, Galveston Storm, Texas, USA

At least 6,000 people died as a result of the Galveston Storm of 1900, when a storm surge flattened most of the wooden buildings.

September 1959, Typhoon Vera, Honshu, Japan

Typhoon Vera was the strongest typhoon ever to hit Japan. It battered the coast and then swept across the island, leaving a trail of devastation and 5,000 dead.

September 1988, Hurricane Gilbert, Caribbean

Gilbert was a powerful hurricane that formed in 1988 and was the second most intense ever seen. Gilbert created widespread destruction in the Caribbean Sea and the Gulf of Mexico.

August 1992, Hurricane Andrew, Florida, USA

Small but fierce, Hurricane Andrew blasted the west coast of Florida with Category-5 winds. It then ripped across Florida, to become one of the most expensive hurricanes to hit the US.

September 1996, Hurricane Hortense, Caribbean

Hurricane Hortense was a Category-4 hurricane that brought torrential rain and flooding to the Caribbean islands.

October 1998, Hurricane Mitch, Central America

Hurricane Mitch was one of the most powerful hurricanes in one of the worst years since records began. Mitch caused catastrophic damage and flooding in Honduras, Nicaragua and other Central American countries, before hitting the Bahamas and Florida.

September 1999, Hurricane Floyd, Eastern Seaboard, USA

Hurricane Floyd built to a strong Category-4 hurricane, triggering the third largest evacuation in US history.

September 2003, Hurricane Isabel, Eastern Seaboard, USA

Isabel was a deadly hurricane that reached Category-5. It caused a storm surge and damage in North Carolina and Virginia.

August 2005, Hurricane Katrina, Louisiana, USA

Hurricane Katrina was the most destructive and costly storm to hit the United States. It caused a storm surge that flooded New Orleans, making millions homeless and killing 1,800 in the region. The 2005 hurricane season exceeded the record-breaking 1998 season.

October 2005, Hurricane Wilma, Yucatan Peninsula, Mexico

Hurricane Wilma built into the most intense hurricane ever recorded in the Atlantic. It had Category-5 winds and the lowest ever barometric pressure at the eye. It battered Mexico before moving on to Florida.

August 2008, Hurricane Gustav, Texas, USA

Hurricane Gustav built to a Category-4 hurricane and caused the largest evacuation in US history. More than 3 million people fled the expected hurricane.

September 2008, Hurricane Ike, Caribbean

Hurricane Ike's winds battered islands around the Caribbean Sea and Atlantic Basin. Haiti and the islands of Turks and Caicos were worst affected.

Glossary

air pressure also known as barometric pressure or atmospheric pressure, this is the force exerted on the sea or ground by the weight of the air above

barometer an instrument used to measure atmospheric pressure, especially for weather forecasting

breach a break or failure in a defensive wall or barrier

condense make droplets of liquid from a vapour (gas) by cooling

debris rubbish and broken items

equatorial winds warm winds around the equator that follow established patterns

evacuate to leave an area because of danger

evaporate change from a liquid to a gas

eye the central, calm area of a hurricane

eye wall the band of thick cloud around the eye of a hurricane

hemisphere one half of the world

levee a defensive embankment or dyke built to prevent flooding

martial law when a government suspends a country's normal laws and puts the military in charge

meteorologist a person who studies the weather

reconnaissance the exploration or examination of an area to gather information about it

satellite an object that orbits (travels around) a planet

topsoil the layer of soil rich in nutrients in which plants grow

tornado a small, fierce, whirling wind system

torrential very severe

tropical relating to the tropics – the areas just above and below the equator

tropical depression the first stage in the development of a hurricane

vapour gas

vortex a spiralling weather system or mass, like a whirlwind

wind gauge an instrument used to measure the speed of the wind

Further Information

FURTHER READING

Eye Witness: Hurricane and Tornado, by Jack Challoner (Dorling Kindersley, 2004)

Hurricanes, by Seymour Simon (HarperCollins, 2003)

I Survived Hurricane Katrina, 2005, by Lauren Tarshis (Scholastic, 2011)

Inside Hurricanes, by Mary Kay Carson (Sterling, 2010)

WEBSITES

Hurricane and Tropical Storm Facts
www.nhc.noaa.gov

Hurricane Information
www.weatherwizkids.com/weather-hurricane.htm

National Geographic
www.nationalgeographic.com/forcesofnature

Index